To Steven.
from his Dad
6—78

Sports Illustrated
FOOTBALL: QUARTERBACK

The Sports Illustrated Library

BOOKS ON TEAM SPORTS

Baseball	Football: Defense	Ice Hockey
Basketball	Football: Offense	Soccer
Curling: Techniques and Strategy	Football: Quarterback	Volleyball

BOOKS ON INDIVIDUAL SPORTS

Badminton	Horseback Riding	Table Tennis
Fly Fishing	Judo	Tennis
Golf	Skiing	Track and Field: Running Events
Handball	Squash	

BOOKS ON WATER SPORTS

Powerboating	Small Boat Sailing
Skin Diving and Snorkeling	Swimming and Diving

SPECIAL BOOKS

Dog Training	Training with Weights
Safe Driving	

Sports Illustrated
FOOTBALL:
QUARTERBACK

By BUD WILKINSON

Illustrations
by Robert Handville

J. B. LIPPINCOTT COMPANY
Philadelphia and New York

U.S. Library of Congress Cataloging in Publication Data

Wilkinson, Charles Burnham.
    Sports illustrated football: quarterback.

    (The Sports illustrated library)
    1. Quarterback (Football)   I. Handville, Robert.
II. Sports illustrated (Chicago)   III. Title.
IV. Title: Football, quarterback.
GV951.3.W54   796.33'22   75–17678
ISBN–0–397–01097–4
ISBN–0–397–01105–9 (pbk.)

Photograph on page 8: Neil Leifer.
Photograph on page 10: Sheedy & Long.
Photographs on pages 12, 78 and 90: Heinz Kluetmeier.
Photographs on pages 20, 34, 50 and 93: Walter Iooss, Jr.
Photograph on page 88: John Iacono.

Contents

Sports Illustrated
FOOTBALL:
QUARTERBACK

Introduction

QUARTERBACK is the glamour position in modern football. At all levels of competition, the skill of the quarterback is the key factor in the success of the offense. His ability to handle the ball is an integral part of the running game, and his ability to throw is a crucial part of the passing attack. If the quarterback is limited in any phase of play, the offense of his team is similarly limited.

The quarterback, to be effective, must have adequate size, good vision, quick reactions and a strong, authoritative voice. He must have a keen mind to be able to sense changes in the defense and to select plays accordingly, for even if most of the plays are called by the coaching staff, the quarterback must be prepared to change each call, if necessary, at the line of scrimmage.

For the sake of simplicity, the diagrams in the book use one offensive formation: two wide receivers and split running backs. Also, the familiar "Oklahoma" pattern with the 5-2 front is the basic defensive alignment used.

9

The detailed descriptions of the quarterback's techniques assume he is right-handed. Left-handed readers simply reverse the order in which they move their feet, hands and arms.

This book details the fundamental instruction of a quarterback. It is not meant for the highly sophisticated coach or player but is intended as a basic text for the young player, for the coaches of young players, and for fans who desire a more intimate knowledge of the quarterback's job.

1
Physical Requirements

THE IDEAL QUARTERBACK would stand over six feet and weigh over 200 pounds. He would have the running ability of O. J. Simpson and the throwing arm and judgment of Johnny Unitas. The height would enable him to see over rushing linemen on pass plays. The weight would give him durability. His ability to run would give the ground game a priceless new dimension, and his passing would balance the offense.

But there is a lot more to quarterbacking than conforming to a set of abstract standards. Eddie LeBaron, quarterback for the Washington Redskins during the '50s, was only five foot nine, but his skill and ability made him the equal of any quarterback of his time. Bob Griese, who is under six feet tall and weighs only 190 pounds, must certainly be considered among the best professional quarterbacks today. And while both Terry Bradshaw of the Pittsburgh Steelers and Roman Gabriel of the Philadelphia Eagles conform to the physical ideal better than either LeBaron or Griese, they are no more effective in playing the position.

BASIC REQUIREMENTS

Quickness is the essential ingredient. Since the quarterback controls the ball on nearly every play, his speed determines the speed with which any play can attack and penetrate the defense. Some coaches, particularly in the pros, limit the quarterback's running, usually because they fear he will be injured. In my opinion, a running quarterback is not nearly as likely to be injured as one who cannot run. The most vulnerable man on the field is a quarterback standing motionless in the pocket, waiting to throw the ball, for should his blocking break down he is a sitting duck. I rarely recall an option quarterback's being injured while running an option-type play. Fran Tarkenton is one of the few professional quarterbacks who has never been injured, and Tarkenton has been scrambling for twenty years.

In college football, the most consistently successful teams have been, in recent years, those which allowed the quarterback to run, not just as a last resort on a broken play but by design. In the professional ranks, the scramblers, such as Griese, Tarkenton and Roger Staubach, by using their ability to carry the ball, come up with key plays that enable their teams to win championships. Of course, the ability to throw is of vital importance, but the tendency is to emphasize the quarterback as passer and ignore his possibilities as a runner.

The most overlooked physical requirement of a quarterback is exceptional vision, which includes good depth perception as well as good peripheral vision. The quarter-

14

back's ability to see the movements of defenders and of his own men is essential to the success of both running and passing plays.

The quarterback must also possess a strong, commanding voice, loud enough to be heard even when crowd noise is high, so that his team can hear the starting count and any audible plays called at the line of scrimmage.

DEVELOPMENTAL DRILLS

Maximizing Size and Strength

While hereditary factors determine the build of any young man, proper diet and body-building exercises will help him attain his maximum physical potential. A balanced diet is the key. If a youngster tends to be too thin, dietary supplements may be needed to add weight. If he tends toward obesity, limiting calorie intake while maintaining a high level of proteins and vitamins may alleviate the problem. In all cases, before a young man begins a drastic dietary program he should consult a physician.

In conjunction with proper diet, potential quarterbacks should engage in a balanced program of weight lifting and isometric exercises. Weight lifting strengthens the muscles during the entire process of raising and lowering the weights, while isometrics develops muscles in one position of tension. The two forms of exercise should be combined for best results.

Developing Quickness and Speed

One of the best drills for developing quickness and speed is running an obstacle course.

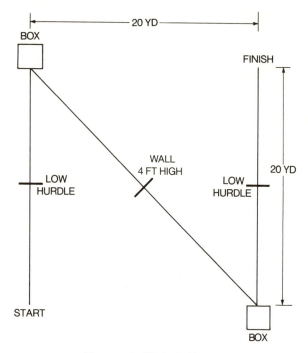

Diagram 1. Obstacle Course

While holding a peg in his left hand, the runner sprints the first leg of the N-shaped course, jumping the hurdle. At the end of the first leg, he deposits the peg in the box, runs to the wall, and scales it. Completing the diagonal leg, he takes a peg from the box with his right hand and sprints the final leg, going over the second hurdle. He then runs the course in reverse. His goal is to improve his combined time for the two complete runs.

In addition to running the obstacle course, a potential quarterback should practice running sideways, both to the left and to the right, crossing his legs while keeping his shoulders parallel, and also running backward, doing both at top speed. He should also do wind sprints of 20, 30 and 40 yards.

16

Developing Ball-Carrying Ability

Truly great ball carriers are born, not made, but any player can improve his running ability by learning a few basic moves and practicing them until they become second nature.

The Side Step: Run at a fixed object such as a bush or tree. To sidestep to the left, plant your right foot, spring laterally, then drive off your left foot along the original course. To sidestep to the right, plant your left foot, spring to the right, and drive off your right foot.

The Cross-Over Step: Approach a fixed object, plant your left foot firmly, and swing your right leg in front of and across your left knee as far as possible. Swing your left leg out from behind your right and take the next step forward, driving off your right foot. To cross over to the right, plant your right foot, cross over with your left leg, swing your right leg around, and drive off your left foot.

The Pivot: Again, run at a fixed object, plant your left foot, and spin to the left by pulling your right leg in behind your left and springing off your left foot onto your right. Make sure to turn at least 180 degrees in this step. Complete the pivot by planting your right foot and spinning once again, swinging your left foot around and driving off your right foot along the original course. The pivot to the right is performed in the same manner, exchanging the directions for left and right feet.

If a blocking dummy is available, you can do these drills with a *stiff arm*. Extend the arm that is not holding the ball outward, with the elbow locked. As you make contact with the dummy, push off with your hand while executing the appropriate foot movements.

A ball carrier must react to the movements of defenders. The drill for this requires three dummies or light, movable objects such as cardboard boxes. These should be placed on a line, with about 1 yard separating them. The ball carrier runs directly at the middle dummy. When he is about a yard from contact, a coach, standing behind the dummy, steps quickly into the slot on either side. The runner, reacting to this, breaks through the remaining slot (Diagram 2).

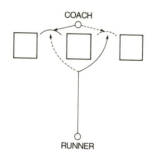

Diagram 2. Break-to-Daylight Drill

You should practice all these drills at half speed until you have learned to perform and coordinate the foot and arm movements. When you have mastered these, gradually increase your speed until you can execute the moves precisely while moving at top speed.

Learning to Throw

The only way to learn to throw is by throwing. The young player should play catch with a friend, warming up at a distance of about 10 yards and gradually increasing the distance to the limits of his strength. Young quarterbacks should be careful not to overextend themselves; trying for too much distance too early can damage the arm. As the player grows toward maturity, his arm will develop naturally and his range and accuracy will improve. In addition to playing catch, three or four young men can alternate in running pass patterns so that the thrower can get practice in leading a receiver.

18

The passer should alternately line the ball and arch it, since quarterbacks must master both types of throws.

Developing Good Vision

Vision, like build, is an inherited quality. Unlike deficiencies of skeleton, however, visual deficiencies can be almost entirely corrected by modern contact lenses, and peripheral vision can be improved by performing simple exercises. Look straight ahead, place your left hand behind your left ear, and gradually bring the hand forward until you can see the movement. (Don't shift your eyes or turn your head.) Then follow the same procedure with your right hand held behind your right ear. Also, try holding one hand above your head or under your chin and performing the exercise from these positions. Frequent practice of these exercises will improve the range and quality of your peripheral vision.

Developing a Strong Voice

According to legend, Demosthenes, the Greek orator, suffered from a speech impediment. To cure his problem he practiced speaking with his mouth full of pebbles until, even so hampered, he could articulate clearly. The young quarterback can achieve similar results (without resort to pebbles) by reading aloud and saying any of the old tongue-twisters like "Peter Piper picked a peck of pickled peppers."

In addition to having good articulation, the quarterback should have a *loud* voice. Being soft-spoken is no crime, except for a quarterback on the field. Very often it is a result of shyness. One great quarterback, Gene Calame, who played for Oklahoma University in the early '50s, had this problem. Both his parents were mutes, which gave Calame an uncanny perceptive ability but also a decided tendency toward soft-spokenness. To overcome this characteristic, Calame would go to a secluded spot and practice calling signals at the top of his lungs. Even the shiest quarterback can learn to shout when there is no one around to hear him.

2
Putting the Ball in Play

THE QUARTERBACK must realize that the way he acts before the team reaches the line of scrimmage is as important as the way he performs after the snap. A play does not begin when the quarterback calls the snap signal; it begins the moment he enters the huddle.

The quarterback should not enter the huddle until it is fully formed. Before entering, he should have decided on the formation, the play, and the starting count. In a voice distinct enough to eliminate uncertainty but low enough to avoid being overheard by the opposition, the quarterback calls his play. (If a player is not sure of the call he should say "Check," requesting that the quarterback repeat it. This is the only time a voice other than the quarterback's should be heard in the huddle.) The quarterback should delay a second or two after calling the signals to be certain that the other players have understood. He then says "Break," and the team moves quickly to the line of scrimmage and assumes the required formation.

The quarterback positions himself behind the center. He looks over the defense to make sure that, either by design or by accident, they have not set themselves in an alignment that would doom his play to failure. If the defense is stacked against the play, the quarterback should change it by calling an audible, repeating the new call twice, if necessary, once to the left and once to the right, to be sure all his players have heard. Once he is sure that the defense is not stacked against the play he says, "Ready, set," and proceeds with the starting count.

THE STARTING COUNT

There are two kinds of starting counts, rhythmic and nonrhythmic. In a rhythmic count, the quarterback calls numbers at an even tempo, the ball being snapped on the number that he has called in the huddle. The weakness of this type of count is that the offensive players may tend to anticipate the "go" signal by leaning, which can result either in a penalty or in telegraphing the signal to the defense.

In the nonrhythmic count, a combination of two sounds, such as "set-go" or "hut-two," is used. The number called in the huddle refers to the number of the combination in the series, and the ball is snapped on the first, second or third combination. The quarterback makes no attempt to count rhythmically, and the only advance warning the offensive team has is the first sound of the combination. The offensive players charge when they hear this first sound and, allowing for reaction time, they are actually moving with the second portion of the double count. Since there is no rhythm to the count, offensive players will not tend to lean. The nonrhythmic count also eliminates the need for all the team's quarterbacks to use the same rhythm.

22

THE SNAP

The exchange of the ball between the center and the quarterback must be practiced until it is completely automatic. After the center is in position, the quarterback sets up close behind him, placing his hands beneath the center's crotch with the forefinger of the right hand in the middle. The back of the right hand should exert enough pressure so that the center can be certain of the hand's exact positioning. The thumb and heel of the left hand are placed against the corresponding parts of the right hand, making a pocket for the ball (Fig. 1). The quarterback must be so close to the

Figure 1. Position of Hands for Receiving Snap

center that his hands can move forward as the center charges, maintaining contact until he has grasped the ball firmly (Fig. 2).

Figure 2. Stance for Receiving Snap

The center should place the ball in the quarterback's hands with the laces along the second joints of the fingers, already in proper throwing position, thus eliminating the need to reposition the ball and reducing the risk of fumbles (Fig. 3).

24

Figure 3. Placement of Ball in Receiver's Hands

The quarterback, while receiving the ball, should be taking his first step. By receiving the ball and taking the step simultaneously, the quarterback gains a split-second advantage over the defense. If he delays that first step until after he has received the ball, he will lose time, which can make the difference between a successful play and a failure (Fig. 4).

Figure 4. Quarterback Taking First Step

The correct execution of the exchange is fundamental to good ball handling. There is no point in teaching any other aspect of play execution until the quarterback has learned to receive the ball accurately, properly and surely *every time*.

3
Fundamentals of Ball Handling

UNLESS THE PLAY calls for the quarterback to keep the ball, the quarterback's job, after taking the snap, is to transfer possession to another player, either by means of a hand-off or a pass. Obviously, to throw the ball through the air, either forward or laterally, requires practice and skill. Making a sure, clean hand-off requires just as much practice and skill.

THE HAND-OFF

When the quarterback is to hand the ball off to another player, he begins well before the actual transfer. As soon as he turns away from the center, he should focus his attention on the receiving player's farther hip, instead of looking at his whole body; the receiving player should raise his elbow to be sure that the quarterback gets a clear view of the small target. The quarterback then lays the ball into the cradle formed by the receiving player's arms *as gently as possible* (Fig. 5).

27

Figure 5. The Hand-off

A. Quarterback focuses on receiving back's hip.

B. The ball is placed gently in the receiving player's arms.

C. The quarterback releases the ball only when he is sure the runner has control of it.

D. After hand-off, the quarterback avoids looking at the runner.

It is important that the quarterback time his movements to coordinate with those of the man who will get the ball. The ball carrier must watch the defenders in the area. As he runs his assigned course, the quarterback *must bring the ball to him*. If for some reason the quarterback does not feel that he can make a clean, accurate hand-off, he should keep the ball, turn upfield, and gain what yardage he can.

THE FAKE HAND-OFF

When the quarterback is to fake a hand-off and keep the ball himself, the faking back *must adjust his course to the*

Figure 6. The Fake Hand-off

A. Quarterback begins fake by looking at the back being faked to.

B. After faking hand-off, quarterback hides the ball on far hip, trails the back with empty hand, and follows him with his eyes.

quarterback's to ensure a close mesh and a successful fake.

As he goes by, the quarterback makes the motions of the hand-off but, instead of releasing the ball, slides it back against his own stomach, holding it with the hand that would naturally be out of sight of the defense (the left hand on hand-offs to the left, the right hand on hand-offs to the right), while his other hand stays in contact with the faking back's stomach, adding to the illusion that the ball has actually been transferred. The purpose of a fake is to fool the defense, and it is vitally important that the quarterback make the hand-off fake appear real. The quarterback should use his hands and eyes to heighten the illusion of the fake.

C. Fake is maintained while dropping back by watching the runner and keeping the ball hidden against stomach.

D. Quarterback keeps the ball until the last moment, when setting up ready to pass.

The vital detail here is eye contact: as the faking back continues past the quarterback, the quarterback should watch him intently, following the plunging back's progress into the line as if the fate of the play rode with him (Fig. 6E).

Figure 6E. Maintaining eye contact with faking back is a key element in a successful fake.

DEVELOPMENTAL DRILLS

The best way to practice ball handling is to have a center snap the ball, so that the quarterback can practice the starting count, taking the snap, and all subsequent ball handling at the same time. If a center is unavailable, the quarterback can begin the drills by simply slapping the ball between his hands.

32

To practice the hand-off, the quarterback and the receiving back should line up in proper position relative to each other. After the starting count and the snap, the back runs his course at full speed while the quarterback makes his moves. This drill should be repeated for each receiver on all plays where the back gets a hand-off from the quarterback.

This drill should include, in addition to the quarterback, all the backs who will either fake or receive the hand-off. If, for example, the play calls for the quarterback to fake one hand-off and give to the second man through, the drill requires both those backs in addition to the quarterback and the center. If the play calls for the quarterback to retain the football for a pass or run, one additional back will be sufficient.

In the hand-off, the quarterback *follows the lead of the receiver*, timing his motions with those of the back approaching him. In a fake (and in a fake drill), the faking back *adjusts his course to that of the quarterback*, and the quarterback goes through the motions as described. While it is the quarterback's responsibility to adjust his motion only to the course of the back who will actually receive the ball, he must *act* as though the faking back were all-important. The quarterback, besides going through the physical motions of the drill, must practice maintaining eye contact with the faking back to mislead the defense as long as possible.

4
Fundamentals
of Passing

DIFFERENT QUARTERBACKS use slightly different grips for throwing, but generally speaking, the larger the quarterback's hand is, the easier it is for him to grasp the ball. The object is to control the ball with the fingertips.

THE GRIP

The laces of the ball should rest along the second joints of the fingers. The fingers themselves are slightly spread, with the thumb in a natural position on the other side of the ball.

35

The football is actually held on the joints of the fingers and the first joint of the thumb and is controlled by the fingertips (Fig. 7). The ball should *not* be palmed.

Figure 7. Normal Grip

Passers who have a tendency to throw the ball with the point down can overcome this difficulty by spreading the forefinger away from the second finger and placing it just under the point of the ball. With this grip the tip of the forefinger is the last part of the hand to touch the football as it is thrown and serves to keep the nose of the ball up (Fig. 8).

Figure 8. Spread Finger Grip

Passers with unusually large hands may hold the ball with the laces across the upper part of the palm, thus gripping the ball with the first joint of the thumb and the fingertips to obtain the desired delicate control (Fig. 9).

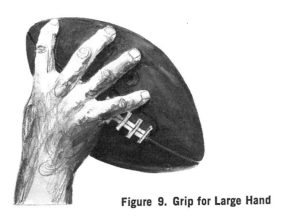

Figure 9. Grip for Large Hand

Figure 10. Right and Wrong Grips

A. Grasp ball with fingers.

B. Never palm the ball.

THE THROW

To begin the throw, the quarterback brings the ball back behind his right ear (if he is throwing with the right hand) as he steps forward with his front foot directly toward his target (Fig. 11A), but keeps his weight on the rear foot. The target is *not* the intended receiver, but rather the place where the receiver should be when the ball gets there. The quarterback winds up, drawing his throwing arm back, and lifts the other arm for balance (11B). His weight is still back.

The ball is thrown by bringing the hand and arm sharply forward with an overhand motion, letting the ball rotate off the palm to the fingertips to impart a spiral, adding stability in flight (11C). Power is gained by rapidly shifting weight to the forward foot. At the end of the throwing motion, the palm should be open and facing the ground, the hand about shoulder height (11D).

Figure 11. The Throwing Sequence

A   B

The throw should be made as quickly as possible. If the passer wastes time winding up, the defense will have time to react and move toward the target before the ball has even left the quarterback's hand. This can, however, be made to work to the quarterback's advantage.

Since the quarterback knows the routes his receivers will be running, he does not need to look at them, nor does he need to see the target directly until just before delivering the ball. By concentrating on another, false target—perhaps on the other side of the field, or deep instead of short—the quarterback can execute an "eye fake" and "look the defense away" from his actual target. He can see the real target area with his good peripheral vision at the same time. This technique can be tremendously effective, especially when it is combined with a fake pass. Immediately before throwing, the quarterback should see the defensive men in the receiver's area, to be certain no one is in position to intercept the pass.

C   D

To fake a pass, the quarterback starts his motion in the normal manner (Fig. 12A), stepping forward with his front foot and moving his arm sharply (12B), but stops the release of the ball with his free hand. Both hands should be used in faking to minimize the risk of accidental release. After stopping the ball, the quarterback brings it back in to his body

Figure 12. Faking a Pass

A   B

(12C), at the same time sliding his back foot forward so that once again he is in the ready position, prepared to deliver the ball quickly to the intended target before the defense has a chance to read the fake and react. Even if the defense is not fooled by the fake, this tactic prevents the secondaries from committing themselves quickly, giving a receiver a split-second advantage in his effort to get open.

C

PASSING TRAJECTORIES

There are two distinct types of pass trajectories. One, the on-line or "clothesline," is used when there is no defensive man between thrower and receiver who could intercept the ball. The important factor here is speed; that is, getting the ball directly to the receiver before a defender has the opportunity to move in on the line and deflect or intercept the pass. The quarterback delivers the ball on a straight, flat line so that it will be in the air the minimum amount of time and give the defenders little chance to cover.

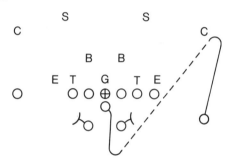

Diagram 3. Lined Pass
No defender between passer and receiver.

The other type, the lofted pass, is thrown when a defender is between the quarterback and the intended receiver and the ball must be thrown over him. In situations where the ball must be arched over a defender, the height of the arch will depend upon the pass route of the receiver. The ball should be thrown high enough so that the receiver can run under it. Excellent receivers will time their movements to the ball by altering the route slightly so that they always catch the ball while reaching up as high as possible and while running at full speed.

Depending on the actual play pattern, there are variations in lined and lofted throws. The ability to make these adjustments can be achieved only through constant practice.

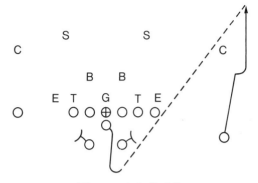

Diagram 4. Lofted Pass
Ball must be thrown over a defender.

The quarterback must strive to develop a "touch" which will enable him to make the path of the ball conform to the needs of the play being run.

THE DROP-BACK PASS

The quarterback must learn to throw both from a set, or ready, position and also while on the run. In each case the throwing action is fundamentally the same.

The quarterback receives the ball from the center as he does on all other plays. It is important that he do nothing different before the snap of the ball when the play is a pass instead of a run; wiping one's hands or looking downfield more intently than usual may be tip-offs that can help an alert defense key on the play.

On drop-back passes, the quarterback moves back from the line of scrimmage as fast as possible. Generally he will drop deeper for long passes than for short ones, so that it will take more time for defensive linemen to reach him and give the receivers additional time to get downfield. Some coaches, however, set the depth the same for all plays, usually about 6 yards behind the line of scrimmage; this way, the offensive linemen can practice protecting one area rather than varying positions.

43

The quarterback makes the drop in one of two ways. He can run backward or he can turn and run into position (Fig. 13A) and turn back again. Running backward gives the quarterback the advantage of being able to see the entire field of play—his receivers and the defenders—constantly. By turning, he can see only half the field and could be tackled on the blind side or could miss a defensive maneuver he might otherwise detect. On the other hand, most men can turn and run much more quickly than they can backpedal and will therefore get set up more quickly with less chance of stumbling and have a longer period of time to watch the defense while actually in position to throw the ball.

When the quarterback has dropped to the desired depth,

Figure 13. The Drop-Back Pass

A

he assumes the ready position (13B), holding the ball in both hands, slightly lower than shoulder height, and spreading his feet about half a yard apart, with the heel of one foot (the left foot for a right-handed passer) a few inches in front of the toes of the other. Most of his weight should be on his rear foot (13C). As he delivers the ball, the quarterback steps forward with his front foot along the line of the pass (13D).

B   C   D

THE RUNNING PASS

The technique of throwing on the run varies only slightly from that of the drop-back pass. A right-handed quarterback rolling out to his right can throw the ball while moving laterally or backward (Fig. 14A), but if he can manage to get

D   C

outside the defensive end, to "turn the corner" before he makes the throw, he will be heading upfield as he releases the ball (14B). Even though he is moving, he can make his delivery in precisely the same manner as on a drop-back pass, releasing the ball while driving off his right foot onto his left (14C and D).

Figure 14. The Running Pass, Right

B   A

When running to his left to throw, a right-handed quarterback *must get turned upfield* to have proper position and momentum to throw the ball accurately (Fig. 15). If he doesn't turn, his momentum will be away from the pass, decreasing both accuracy and distance. In either case, the quarterback must be certain he is still behind the line of scrimmage when he lets go of the ball.

Figure 15. The Running Pass, Left

A

B

C   D

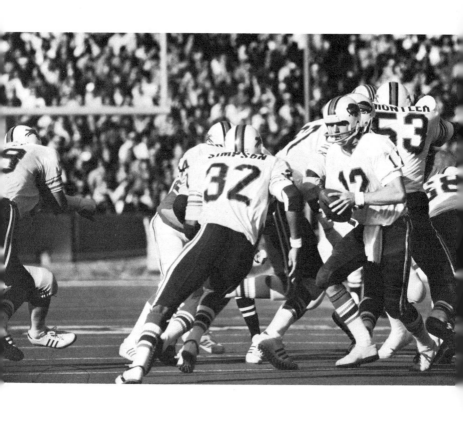

DEVELOPMENTAL DRILLS

The most effective way of strengthening the arm and wrist muscles used in throwing is to throw. To gain additional strength, you can devise a system of weights and pulleys to put added load on the arm as you go through your throwing motion. Another way of doing this is to play catch with a weighted ball. To improve the wrist muscles, squeeze a small rubber ball thirty or forty times three or four times a day.

To improve passing accuracy, the most effective training is to throw the ball, throw the ball, and then throw the ball some more. In addition to playing catch with an actual receiver, you can suspend an old tire from a tree limb or a goalpost by means of a rope and practice throwing the ball through the hole from various angles and distances—from the ready position and while running.

Before each throw, practice getting from your set position behind the center into the ready position and throwing the ball as quickly as possible.

5

Basics
of Play Execution

IN MODERN FOOTBALL there are many variations in offensive formations and individual plays, but in a basic sense running plays can be separated into three types, those designed to hit outside, those designed to go inside, and those designed to fool or misdirect the defense.

BASIC RUNNING PLAYS

On running plays where he will not carry the ball, the quarterback's primary job is to transfer possession of the ball from the center to the designated running back with the maximum speed and the minimum risk. Once the ball has been successfully handed off, the quarterback becomes a faker. He must avoid doing anything that might tip off defenders, such as following the actual runner with his eyes, while he fakes other actions—hand-offs to any backs remaining in the backfield, roll-outs, or passes—to confuse the defense, if only for a second. In so doing, the quarterback helps the play in progress and may also set the scene for a future play.

A quarterback who is a reasonably accomplished runner is a tremendous asset. He is a potential running back, and therefore, even in a formation which has only one set back, the defense cannot afford to key too heavily on that back as a runner or assume that the play will be a pass. There are plays in which the quarterback's ability to run puts the defense in a quandary, for whatever move they make will be wrong. Such a play is the option.

The Option Play

The basic strategy of the option play is very simple: it involves running two potential ball carriers (the quarterback and a running back) at a single defender (the defensive end), forcing the defender to commit himself to stopping one of them, and then transferring the ball to the other. As the quarterback takes the snap, his first act is to *look at the defensive end*. The offensive line, firing out strongly

Diagram 5. The Option Play

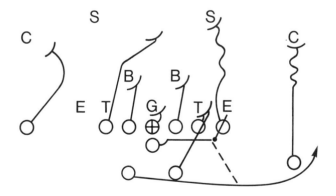

A. Quarterback pitches.

Diagram 5. The Option Play (cont'd)

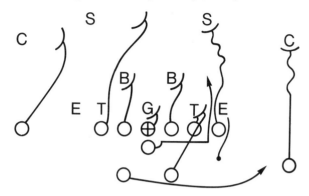

B. Quarterback keeps.

after the snap, gives him room to run along parallel to the line and, if possible, slightly forward. The trailing back moves with him, about 5 yards deep. The quarterback, approaching the defensive end, holds the ball numeral high. If the end moves to stop him, the quarterback simply flips the ball to his trailer and turns upfield. The quarterback must keep the throw shoulder high, so the receiver will be able to field it even if it is not directly on target (Fig. 16).

Figure 16. The Option Pitch. The key to the option is the defensive end. If he commits himself to tackling the quarterback, the quarterback should pitch the ball to his trailing back.

A

B

C

D

Should the defensive end penetrate to contain the trailer, the quarterback merely keeps the ball, faking the pitchout to make the end commit himself further, and cuts directly upfield (Fig. 17).

The option play is easily executed and usually successful if the defenders except the end are blocked, because whatever move the end makes will be wrong. The success of the play depends on the quarterback's ability to react quickly to the movement of the defensive end. When the quarterback is in doubt about the end's play—if, for example, the end hangs back and refuses to commit himself—the quarter-

Figure 17. The Option Keep. If the defensive end penetrates to contain the trailing back, the quarterback should fake the pitch and cut through the hole.

A

back should keep the ball and turn upfield, assuring a gain of at least 3 yards, since he will be tackled from behind and can fall forward. He also avoids the risk of a fumble on the pitchout. Remember that a ball thrown laterally is a free ball if it is not caught. The quarterback should remain alert to the possibility of a mishandle on this and every other play.

B

C

The Triple-Option Play

The strategy of the option against the end added to the option of giving the ball to the faking back results in the famed "triple option" play (Fig. 18). The quarterback now watches two defensive men in sequence, the tackle and the end.

Figure 18. The Triple Option. The first option the quarterback has is to fake or give to the running back. If the quarterback fakes to his running back, he then keeps (D) or pitches (E).

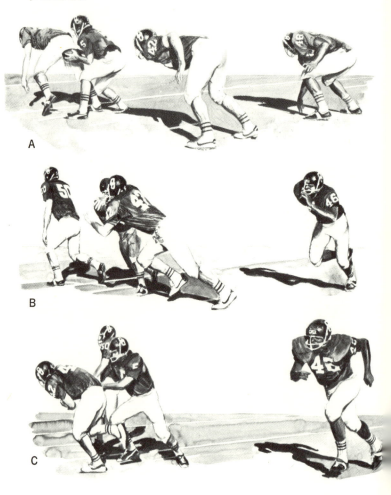

A

B

C

D

E

Taking the snap, the quarterback places the ball on the hip of the onside running back, moving with the back while he takes his second step toward the line of scrimmage and to the outside, while *keeping his eyes* on the defensive *tackle*.

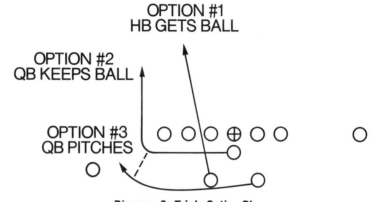

Diagram 6. Triple-Option Play
Defensive reaction determines quarterback's choice.

If the tackle crosses the line of scrimmage, the quarterback allows the running back to keep the ball. Should the tackle cross the line, the running back is assured of a solid gain. If the tackle closes to stop the running back, the quarterback retains the ball and continues on down the line of

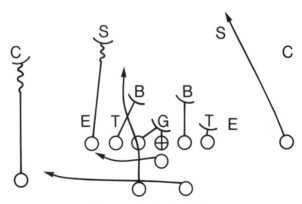

Diagram 7. Triple Option
A. Quarterback gives ball to halfback.

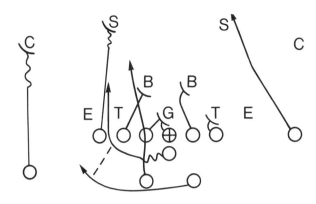

Diagram 7. Triple Option (cont'd)
B. Quarterback keeps or pitches.

scrimmage, running the rest of the play just like the normal option. When in doubt as to the actions of the tackle, the quarterback should give the ball to the first back, for this runner has momentum, is heading toward the line of scrimmage, and will probably make some yardage. The quarterback must always continue on after the hand-off and fake the option play.

The Quarterback Sweep

Both the option and the triple option use the quarterback as a running *threat*, but there are other plays which use the quarterback as a runner from the beginning, with no intention of giving the ball to anyone else. Such a play is the quarterback sweep.

The quarterback sweep is a powerful, exceptionally safe play. It is powerful because two running backs lead the play and provide blocking; it is safe because no exchanges are required after the snap.

Figure 19. The Quarterback Sweep

A

B

C

Proper footwork is important. The quarterback takes the snap and steps back and out with his right foot (Fig. 19A). If the play is being run to the right, he steps back and across with his left foot and moves away from the line of scrimmage at about a 45-degree angle to a depth of about 5 yards, thus permitting the second running back to cross in front of him (19B). Once the back has crossed, the quarterback straightens out and raises the ball to fake the pass (19C).

D

He should be watching the block that the lead running back is putting on the defensive end. If the end moves slowly across the line and stays in tight, the back will be able to hook the defender in with his block. The quarterback and the second blocker move around to the outside of all defenders except the cornerback, who should have been blocked or effectively faked out of position by the flanker.

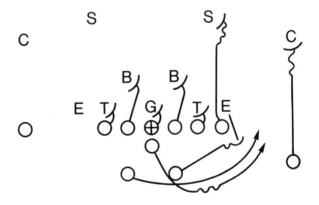

Diagram 8. Quarterback Sweep with Fake Pass

Diagram 9. Quarterback Sweep

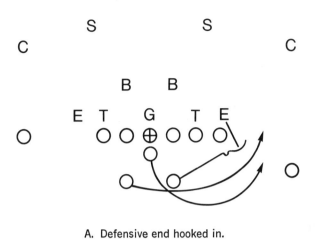

A. Defensive end hooked in.

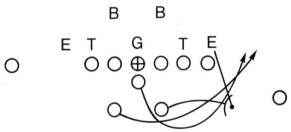

B. Defensive end blocked out.

BASIC PASSING PLAYS

The Drop-Back Pass

Basic passing plays, like basic running plays, require the offense to adjust to the play of the defense *after* the ball is snapped. In this sense, basic passing plays are a logical extension of option plays. As in the option, the quarterback must watch the actions of key defenders. When he runs the option, he decides whether the actions of the defensive end mean that he or the trailer will be open. In a pass play, the movements of the defenders dictate which receiver will be open.

The quarterback will have a primary receiver to whom he will throw if he can. He will also have secondary receivers to whom he will throw if the primary receiver is covered. Once the quarterback is in his ready position, he looks at the defensive man who is covering his primary receiver. He does *not* look at the receiver. The quarterback knows where the receiver will be; whether or not the receiver will be able to get the ball depends on the actions of the defender. If the quarterback concentrates on the receiver rather than the defender, he may throw a pass that can be broken up or, worse, intercepted. If the primary receiver is covered, the quarterback should look to his secondary receivers.

The type of pass the quarterback will use will depend on the position of the receiver relative to the defense. Some passes are designed to be caught in front of a defender, as shown in Diagram 10. The cornerback is single-covering the wide receiver on the right side. The quarterback looks first at the near-side safety. If the safety is not dropping with the tight end and is, instead, moving to provide double coverage on the flanker, the quarterback can go to his tight end. If, however, the safety has made the correct drop and is covering the tight end, the quarterback shifts his attention to the *defensive* end, who may be moving out along the line instead of rushing, hanging back for a possible interception.

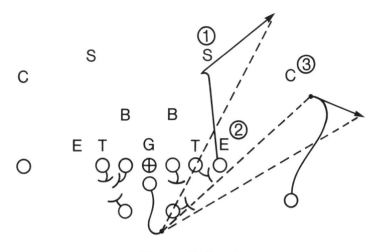

Diagram 10. Pass Play
Wide receiver against defensive corner back.

If the end is rushing or is staying in tight to guard against a possible draw play, the quarterback can look to his primary receiver, the flanker, who is driving downfield, forcing the cornerback to backpedal at full speed. Once the flanker has forced the defender to establish momentum downfield, the flanker can turn back quickly. Since he knows when he will turn and the defender does not, the receiver should be open as the cornerback overcomes his momentum and starts back to the receiver, who will, of course, be moving away from the defender and toward the ball. The pass called for in this situation is of the sharp, clothesline variety. The quarterback must time this throw so that the ball leaves his hand just before the receiver makes his cut. If the receiver is turning toward the center of the field, the quarterback should throw the ball leading him that way. If the receiver is turning toward the sideline, the pass should be thrown to the outside.

This is the correct technique for hitting a receiver who is in front of the defender.

Sometimes the receiver will be behind the defender. This is an occasion for the lofted type of throw. The completion of this kind of pass depends less on split-second timing and more on the ability of the receiver to run a pattern which fools the defender. The quarterback fakes a clothesline throw to the wide receiver, as shown in Diagram 11. The fake of the throw combined with the receiver's fake sideline cut should pull the cornerback up to cover against the short pass. On his third step toward the sideline, however, the flanker turns again and runs a flag pattern. The tight end, running a pattern inside, should pull the safety man in so

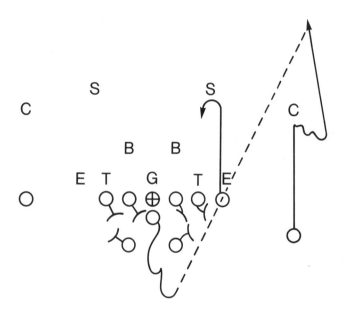

Diagram 11. Pass Play
Ball faked short, then thrown deep.

that there is nothing between the flanker and the goal line but yard stripes. It is the quarterback's job to get him the ball.

The pass should be lofted on a high trajectory to the outside along the sidelines so that the near-side safety, who may not have been completely deceived by the tight end's inside pattern, will not be able to get to it. The play now becomes a footrace between the cornerback and the wide receiver. The receiver hopes to get behind the defender and runs under the ball, taking it over his inside shoulder.

The Play-Action Pass

The play-action pass is designed to look exactly like a running play. When the defense commits itself immediately to stop the run, a pass from the same pattern will usually be open.

The defense is kept honest because the play-action pass could be, in reality, a running play or vice versa, and the defense cannot afford to play either the pass or the run entirely. Thus, it cannot commit itself immediately, and this moment of indecision makes both the pass and the run more effective.

On long-yardage situations, when the defense can be fairly certain that a pass will be called, the play-action pass is less effective. If, for example, it is third down and 7, the defense can afford to play first against the pass to prevent a long gain and still have time to move up and stop a runner before he can get a first down. But in any situation where only short yardage is needed, particularly on second down and short yardage, when the ground play is a high probability, play-action passes are highly effective calls.

An example of the play-action type of pass is the counter-pass (Diagram 12), which evolves from the counter-play.

The quarterback fakes to the right running back, and then fakes giving the ball to the second back, looking at him intently as described in Chapter 3. The quarterback must never hurry back to the throwing position. He should move

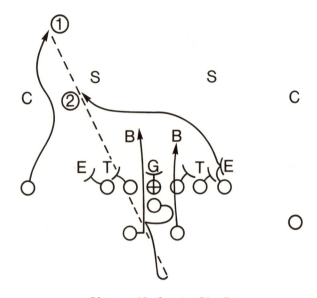

Diagram 12. Counter-Play Pass

at three-quarter speed while looking at the halfback, who is faking carrying the ball. When he is approximately 5 to 6 yards behind the line of scrimmage, the quarterback turns and looks at the defensive safety to his left on the split end's side. If this man has taken the running fake and is coming up, the quarterback throws the ball with a high arch to the split end running the post pattern.

If the left safety has not taken the fake, the quarterback looks at his tight end crossing the field and throws to him as he clears the linebackers, who should be moving up to stop the counter-play fake.

The sprint-out is a play-action pass which is basically an option play. The option, instead of a pitchout, is a forward pass or a run by the quarterback. At the start of the sprint-out, the quarterback moves exactly as he does on a quarterback sweep, allowing the second blocker to cross in front of him, watching the defensive end penetrate and going either

70

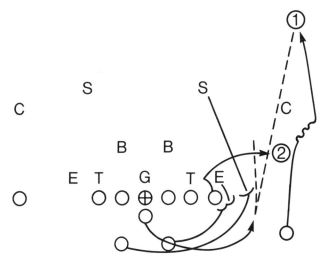

Diagram 13. Sprint-Out Pass

to the outside or the inside, depending on whether the lead blocker can manage to hook the end. At this point the quarterback must *really try to run with the ball.* As can be seen in Diagram 13, there are two defenders to stop the quarterback run, the cornerback and the onside safety. If the cornerback moves up to stop the run, the wide receiver, running down the sidelines, will be open for a lofted pass. If the cornerback sticks with the wide receiver, the safety will have to come up to stop the run, leaving the tight end open. No matter what adjustments the defense makes, either one of two receivers will be in the clear or the quarterback will have room to run and to make considerable yardage on the ground. It is vitally important that the quarterback *try to run and turn upfield* before executing his option to pass. As long as he is moving laterally, the defenders are not greatly pressured. By turning upfield, he forces them to commit themselves.

71

Broken Plays

Pass plays are the safest plays in football, *providing the passer does not throw an interception*. He will rarely make this mistake if he learns to watch the defensive secondary. This calls for poise and courage. He must learn never to force a throw. And he must learn that even if all his receivers are covered, the play is by no means over.

If, after dropping back to his ready position, the quarterback discovers his primary and secondary receivers are effectively covered, he must make the choice either to scramble or to throw the ball away. Throwing the ball away results in the loss of a down. Scrambling has the advantage of a potential gain. The quarterback must learn to weigh this option quickly while under pressure.

The decision to scramble is largely intuitive. Once the quarterback has determined that he has no open receivers, he looks for an opening that will enable him to reach the line of scrimmage. There is no point in scrambling if he is certain he cannot get back that far. While it may seem unlikely that he can find such a hole in the wall of onrushing linemen, there are several factors that improve the quarterback's chances. Defensive linemen are taught to rush the passer with hands held high in the air in order to obscure the quarterback's vision. In this upright position they are more or less off balance and unable to change direction quickly. They are so intent on reaching the quarterback before he can throw the ball that they have great momentum. A quick quarterback can duck past them before they can change direction and pursue. The pass blockers, even if they have been beaten, should be making every effort to force their men outside, creating an opening for the quarterback. As can be seen in Diagram 14, with the defensive pass rush moving toward the quarterback and the defensive secondary making drops with the receivers, an open area is created near the line of scrimmage. If the quarterback can manage to elude the first wave of defenders and reach the

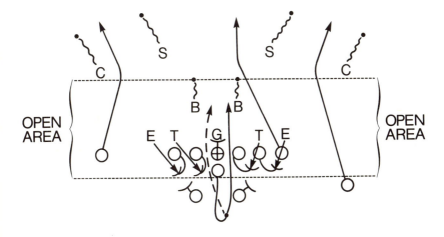

**Diagram 14. Open Area for Quarterback Run After Pass Fake
or When All Receivers Are Covered**

line, he has a good chance of picking up additional yardage.
The important factor is decisiveness. Once the quarterback
has decided to scramble, he must do it without hesitation
and with as rapid an acceleration as possible.

When there is no chance that the quarterback can get
back to the line of scrimmage on a scramble, he must get
rid of the football to avoid being thrown for a loss. The rules
prohibit the quarterback from throwing the ball to an area
that has no receivers. If the referee believes the ball has
been thrown with such intent, he will call a penalty for in-
tentional grounding. When the quarterback decides to throw
the ball away, he must pass it into an area in which there is
an eligible receiver, while keeping it far enough away from
defenders to avoid an interception. This is relatively easy
and safe to do when a receiver is running a pattern near the
sidelines; the quarterback simply throws the ball over the

heads of both receiver and defender, out of bounds. Throwing the ball into the middle of the field requires more care, since the quarterback must throw the ball beyond all members of the defensive secondary (Diagram 15).

The possibility of having to throw the ball away is an added reason for the quarterback to reach his ready position quickly; he will have ample time to consider his options: pass, scramble, or throw the ball away. The final option is to "eat" the football—to allow himself to be tackled. This may be the only sensible alternative during a blitz, when linebackers and members of the defensive secondary desert their normal positions in an all-out effort to reach the quarterback before he can throw the ball. When the quarterback has no time to see the defensive secondary because he is

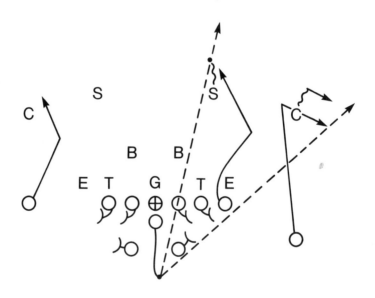

Diagram 15.
Receivers Covered, Quarterback Throws Ball Away

being rushed, his first priority is to tuck the ball away firmly to avoid a fumble.

Since the defense is likely to blitz only on obvious passing downs, the quarterback should be aware of the added risk in these down-and-yardage situations. If he believes the blitz is on, he could counter it by calling a draw play or a screen pass, which may turn the blitz into a defensive disaster. This call can be made either in the huddle or as an audible at the line of scrimmage.

The Screen Pass

Screen passes can be thrown from play-action passes or drop-back passes. All screens operate on the same principles:

1. The receivers start downfield as though this were a normal pass play.

2. The blockers who are not part of the screen make as good a pass protection block as possible.

3. The blockers who will form the screen make the best possible block for two counts and then become good enough actors to convince the defensive men they are blocking that they have beaten the block so they will continue to rush the passer.

4. The receiver of the screen makes his block, then leads the defensive man with whom he is engaged to believe he has beaten the block so he will continue to rush the passer. The receiver then moves out to the flat to receive the pass.

On the screen pass (see Diagram 16), the left guard and center will be the screen men. The left halfback will be the pass receiver.

The split end, the tight end and the wide receiver all run deep patterns to take the secondary defenders back. The right guard, the right tackle and the right halfback all block their men as long and effectively as possible. So does the left tackle.

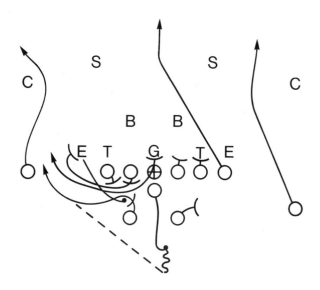

Diagram 16. Screen Pass

The left guard and the center make their blocks for two counts and then glide to the outside. They make their move to the outside about a count and a half before the receiver moves to the outside. The quarterback has already dropped quickly to his ready position. He looks at his split end running the deep flag pattern, then at the tight end running the post pattern, and then at the flanker to his right. By this time the left halfback will have released his block on the end and will be moving to the outside.

The passer now drops back another yard or two, as would be necessary if he were being rushed or needed more time to throw. As he drops back, he should move slightly to his right. As the rushers get close to him, he turns and delivers the ball with as much speed as possible (he may need to loft it over the end) to his halfback, who should catch the ball at a spot approximately 4 yards outside the position where his right tackle originally lined up.

76

The left guard turns downfield and blocks the first man coming from the inside. The center leads downfield and takes the first defensive man who comes to him. The ends and the flanker should block their defensive men as they react when the ball is thrown.

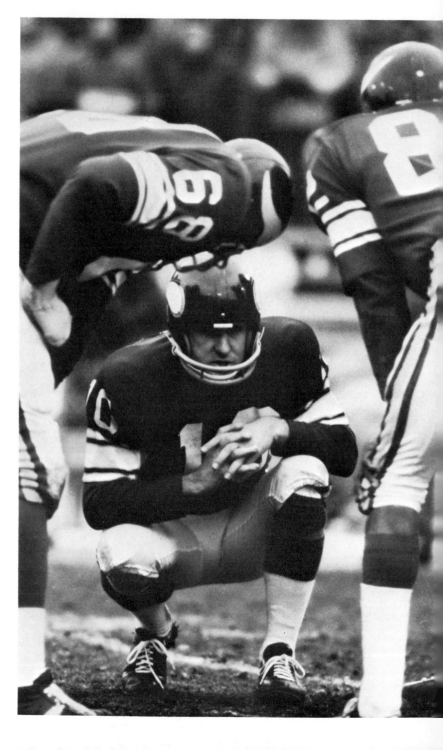

6
Play
Selection

BECAUSE OF THE MANY FACTORS involved in play selection, many coaches prefer to relieve the quarterback of play-calling responsibility and, instead, send in plays from the sidelines. There is, however, another theory about calling plays: If the quarterback is going to have to take responsibility for changing the play by checking signals when the defense is deployed in an alignment that will stop the play cold, he might as well call all the plays. Being in the game, the quarterback may have a better feel for the entire situation, a greater awareness of the mood of the team and so forth, than any sideline observer. Regardless of who calls the play, the fact remains that sooner or later the quarterback will have to check signals and bear the responsibility. He must know how to select plays so that he may take advantage of situations that he sees.

To choose plays wisely, the quarterback must know that *his objective is to make a first down.* He must recognize the strengths and weaknesses of a particular defensive alignment.

He must be aware of the strengths and weaknesses of his teammates. He must also take into account all the factors of his tactical and strategic situation: field position, down and yardage, score, and weather conditions.

PLAY SELECTION BASED ON FIELD POSITION

Many factors contribute to winning a game: an excellent defense that allows no easy breakaway touchdowns, a strong kicking game assuring that the opponent will always get the ball on the exchange in poor field position, and an attack that grinds out yardage steadily and maintains possession of the ball for long periods of time. The obvious objective of offensive football is to put points on the board. However, statistically speaking, the team that controls the ball for the longer time is usually victorious. The quarterback should think of maintaining control, making first downs, keeping the ball. If he thinks exclusively in terms of scoring, he loses his perspective.

From a strategic standpoint, the field is divided into two general areas, the three-down area and the four-down area. In the three-down area of the field the quarterback must recognize that, if he does not make a first down in three plays, he will be forced to kick on fourth down. In the four-down area on fourth down he is close enough to his opponent's goal line either to use a regular offensive play in an attempt to make the first down or to try a field goal. In the three-down area of the field, it is necessary to average 3⅓ yards per play to make the first down. Inside the opponent's 35-yard line in the four-down area, only 2½ yards per play are needed.

The most important single statistic in winning or losing is the number of turnovers made by the offensive team, either by fumbling the ball to the opponents or by throwing the pass interception. The location of these turnovers on the field of play is critical. For this reason the quarterback must understand the relative risk areas as they relate to possible turnovers.

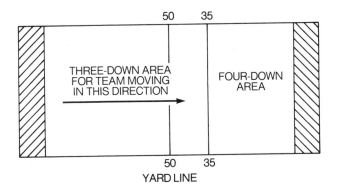

Diagram 17. Quarterback's Three- and Four-Down Areas

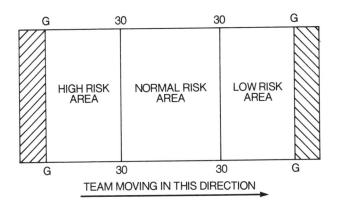

Diagram 18. Quarterback's Relative Risk Areas

DOWN-AND-YARDAGE CONSIDERATIONS

Generally speaking, it is easier to make consistent yardage by hitting straight ahead with all possible speed than by running wide. When the ball carrier is hitting ahead, his momentum guarantees that he will pick up yardage even though he may be tackled on or close to the line of scrimmage. On wide plays, the ball carrier must make a 90-degree turn to get headed upfield, thus losing considerable momentum.

While doing the unexpected is the key to successful quarterbacking, the following rules constitute beginning guidelines for play selection:

● On first down and 10, the quarterback should call a semi-straight-ahead play in an attempt to make 4 or more yards.

● On second down and long yardage (8 or more yards to go), the quarterback should use some type of option or misdirection play in an attempt to confuse the defense and make a minimum of 5 or 6 yards.

● On second down and normal yardage (7 to 5 yards to go), the quarterback should use a play similar to the one called on first down.

● On second down and short yardage (2 yards or less to go), the quarterback has a "waste" down, which means that, even if the play does not succeed, he still can normally make the first down on the next play. Thus he can think in terms of a potential breakaway play, such as a play-action pass, in an attempt to make long yardage.

● On third down and long yardage, the quarterback should use some sort of surprise play, because the defensive team will be thinking in terms of a pass, screen or draw.

● On third down and normal yardage (3 yards or less to go for the first down), the quarterback should use a basic semi-straight-ahead play.

• On third down and short yardage (2 yards or less to go), the quarterback should use his most consistent play.

In the four-down area of the field, the same rules apply as for third down, recognizing that if the team has a competent field-goal kicker, the quarterback will try for a field goal on the fourth down if there is long or normal yardage to go and will use the most consistent gaining play if there is short yardage to go.

TIME, SCORE AND WEATHER CONDITIONS

The field position as just explained and the down yardage are the basic tactical considerations. However, the quarterback must always be aware of the time remaining, the score, and the weather conditions.

Time remaining to play becomes increasingly significant toward the end of any quarter, half, or game. When his team is ahead and time is running out, the quarterback should attempt to maintain possession of the ball and let the clock run. The only exception might be if his team has a very strong wind at its back and the clock indicates that the first or third quarter is about to end. In this circumstance, the quarterback should consider punting the ball to take advantage of the wind and thereby pin the opponent back deep in his territory before losing the wind by the change of goals at the end of the quarter.

When a team is behind, the clock becomes increasingly important. If there is actually sufficient time left—if, say, the team is only one touchdown behind with 6 minutes or more remaining—the quarterback should not panic. He should stick to his game plan and try to pick up a steady succession of first downs to move into scoring position. However, as the time shortens, a team that is behind must recognize that it needs to take more chances by using trick maneuvers in an attempt to fool the defense and break a long-gaining play.

Included in all factors of field position, down, yardage, time and score is the constant element of the weather. There are two major weather conditions that affect the offensive team, wind and rain.

The wind has little or no effect on a running attack, but it can have a marked effect on a passing attack, regardless of whether the wind is with or against a team. When a gale is blowing, the quarterback will find it difficult to complete his passes. With the wind at his back, the ball will "sail," and when he is throwing into the wind, the force will make the ball "hang."

Wet conditions caused by rain affect the running game far more than the passing game. On a wet field it is difficult for ball carriers on wide plays to make the turn upfield, since they always risk slipping. Also, a wet ball, which becomes increasingly wet when it is held against a jersey, is much more likely to be fumbled. On a wet field, pass receivers have the advantage. They know the pattern they will run, while the defenders must adjust to it. The problem of slipping is much more acute for the defender; the receiver usually finds it easier to get open. Also, the ball is usually dried between plays, so the quarterback has a relatively dry ball to throw.

In addition to the tactical considerations, the quarterback must keep in mind the abilities of his own players as he selects his plays. This is particularly important in critical down-and-yardage situations such as third down and 3 to go in the three-down area of the field. Generally speaking, the most dependable ball carrier should get the ball and run over his most consistently effective blockers. The only variation to this rule would be an occasional use of a play which fakes to the "bread-and-butter" back and then gives the ball to another runner. If the bread-and-butter back has made first down on several occasions, the defense will concentrate on him. When this occurs, the fake to him can be an effective change of pace.

WHEN TO PASS

The decision as to whether or not to throw a pass is complicated by the fact that an incomplete pass on first or second down and normal yardage immediately creates a long-yardage situation. This makes it difficult to achieve the basic objective of making a first down.

The best times to throw the ball are a waste-down situation (second down and short yardage to go in the three-down area, or third and short in the four-down area) or on first down after making one or two first downs with the running attack. The quarterback should always try to avoid being forced into a long-yardage situation (third and long in the three-down area, or fourth and long in the four-down area), but when he finds himself in such a situation he should throw, most of the time, since a pass is his only real percentage play to make the first down.

CHECKING SIGNALS

There will certainly be times when, as the quarterback approaches the line of scrimmage, he will see a defensive alignment that is perfectly set to stop the play he has called in the huddle. In this situation, the quarterback must check his signals, calling an audible, so that he will not be running into the strength of the defense.

Regardless of whether the play is called in the huddle or at the line, the quarterback's thinking is much the same: he always attempts to select the best possible play for the tactical situation. Practically speaking, this is an almost impossible job because of the varied play of the defensive team.

Thus, as the quarterback contemplates checking signals, he should be mainly concerned with *avoiding a bad play*.

Diagram 19 indicates an overshifted defense to the right. Against this defense, a wide play to the right will have no chance of gaining; in fact, it will most probably result in a loss. Obviously, the quarterback, having called a sweep to the right, should check signals and direct the play up the middle or to the left side.

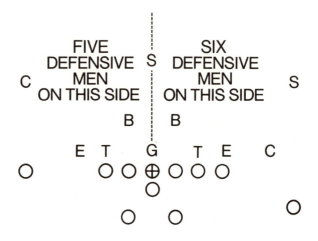

Diagram 19.
Defensive Team Overshifted to the Right

The same theory is true on pass plays. Diagram 20 shows the defense overshifted to the right, with the corner man and the inside safety in position to double-cover the wide receiver. If the quarterback has called a pass to the wide receiver on the right, it will be virtually impossible to complete. He must check signals and call the pass to the split end on his left, who, as the diagram shows, is single-covered.

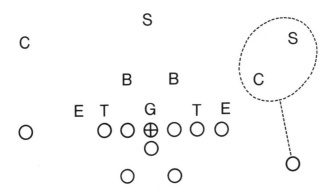

Diagram 20. Defense Double Coverage
Inside corner man and inside safety
can cover wide receiver on right side.

Occasionally, the defensive team may become confused and leave a glaring weakness in the alignment because one of the defensive players has made a mistake in setting up in position. If this occurs, the quarterback obviously should check signals to the open area. However, this is most unlikely to happen, particularly against well organized teams. The major purpose in being able to check signals is the ability to *check away* from a play that is directed at an area of the defense that is overloaded and obviously in position to cause the play to fail.

REACTING TO DEFENSIVE ADJUSTMENTS

Until a quarterback has actually made a play succeed, he is gambling on his ability to use his wits to confuse the defensive team. As long as the defensive team is holding the

offense to no gains or short gains, they will continue to play their assignments steadily without gambling.

When the offense does run a successful play, a gain of 6 yards or more, the defensive players will be conscious of their vulnerability to the play. The first time a gain is made, they may not change their pattern. But if the play succeeds two or three times, they will make a change. *The difference between excellent and average quarterbacking is the ability to anticipate the defensive change one play before the defense makes it.*

7
Leadership

LEADERSHIP BEGINS with personal confidence in one's own ability. The quarterback must work diligently on all physical skills in all departments of play. If he lacks confidence he will be unable to function effectively on decisive plays where the stress factors are at their highest. Only through executing all kinds of plays successfully a number of times in practice will a quarterback develop this type of confidence.

The so-called game-day player is a myth. The idea that an individual can suddenly rise to previously unattained heights because of pressures of the actual game is wishful thinking. Unless the quarterback has practiced enough times to be certain of his ability to make the play, he will not be able to meet the demands of highly charged situations.

When the quarterback is sure he can play his position effectively, his teammates will recognize that he is a true football player: willing and able to block for his teammates,

91

the best-conditioned man on the team, and physically tough and proficient in all fundamentals of play.

The quarterback must also have a personality which is respected by the team so he can get the most out of his players. Every football squad has a wide variety of personalities among its members: some are extroverts and some introverts, with all shadings in between. A quarterback must know and understand his teammates—just as they must believe in him—if the team is to function effectively as a unit. Essentially, the quarterback must ask his team and the individuals in it to respond to the challenge of the situation.

If a player seems to lack confidence, the quarterback should, in a critical situation, say, "Charlie, I know you can make the necessary yardage for us. Men, let's give Charlie all the help he needs," and then call the play.

If a player is inclined to be overconfident, the quarterback can tease him by saying, "Charlie, we need four yards. Your teammates will give you the necessary blocking. Let's see if you can make it."

Two cardinal rules of leadership by the quarterback are: (1) never criticize and (2) be positive, not negative. Criticism by players during a game will break down the team's confidence and prevent it from functioning as a unit. While criticism by the coach and frank discussions among players after practices and games are necessary, critical remarks during the contest itself tend to divide rather than unify.

Positive statements build confidence; negative ones erode performance. If the quarterback tells the ball carrier, "Don't swing too wide before I hand the ball off," he has failed to tell the back which course he *should* take. Instead, he should say, "Run your pattern. I'll get the ball to you," thus setting the proper mental attitude and building the ball carrier's confidence.

All elements of leadership appear in what may have been the most meaningful single occurrence of my coaching career. One season, as we planned the use of our personnel,

our coaching staff recognized that we had a potentially superior quarterback prospect in Bill, a young man who had size, speed, vision, reflexes, strength—all the physical characteristics needed to become a truly great player. Our other quarterback candidate, George, was a boy who was just an average college player with no outstanding physical qualities. Naturally our staff assumed that the gifted athlete would be our quarterback.

We began practice and after four days had our first scrimmage. We started the gifted athlete at quarterback and our team looked miserable. We could not break the huddle cleanly and failed to execute the starting count sharply. We were a sloppy team.

After about ten minutes I substituted and put the second quarterback in charge of the team. Immediately we took on cohesion and looked reasonably effective. I was puzzled.

We practiced three more days and scrimmaged again. Once more we started the potentially great player at quarterback with the same result—our team was disorganized and unable to perform well. I substituted the average athlete at quarterback, and the team immediately looked relatively effective. I was mystified.

After four more days of practice we scrimmaged a third time. We started the gifted athlete at quarterback, and still he was unable to make the team function together effectively. We put in the average athlete, and the team came to life, breaking the huddle sharply, executing the starting count with precision, and moving the ball with consistency. I knew I had to know why.

After practice I stopped our captain and asked him why the team performed better with a less gifted player at quarterback. I can still see the smile on his face when he said, "Coach, it's simple. Bill is trying to show *us* what a great player he is. *We're* trying to make George look good."

The quarterback whose team wants to make him look good has solved the problems of leadership. This attitude can only be earned by the quarterback's ability to perform consistently well in all aspects of the game while always doing his best to make the team more important than himself.